BREAKING UP WITH PEOPLE-PLEASING

By Aubree Henderson & Andrea Seydel

Copyright © 2021 by Aubree Henderson and Andrea Seydel
All rights reserved.
Published and Distributed in Canada by LLH Publishing Inc. **www.andreaseydel.com**
All rights reserved. No part of this book may be reproduced by any mechanical, photographic, or electronic process, or in the form of a phonograph recording, nor may it be stored in a retrieval system, transmitted, or otherwise be copied for public or private use- other than for "fair use" as brief quotations embodied in articles and reviews without prior written permission of the publisher. If you use any of the information in this book for yourself, which is your constitutional right, the author and the publisher assume no responsibility for your actions.
Library of Congress Cataloging-in-Publication Data
Henderson, Aubree and Seydel, Andrea
Breaking Up with People Pleasing\Aubree Henderson and Andrea Seydel
1.Non Fiction Mental Health -2. Non-Fiction-Self-Help-Motivation & Inspiration
ISBN: 978-1-990461-09-5

1st Printing: June 2021. Printed in Canada
Editor and Proofreader: Lindy Bailey

Publisher's Note & Author DISCLAIMER
This publication is designed to provide accurate and authoritative information concerning the subject matter covered. It is sold to understand that the publisher and author are not engaging in or rendering any psychological, medical, or other professional services. If expert assistance or counselling is needed, seek the services of a competent medical professional. For immediate support, call your local crisis line.
BE WELL

TABLE OF CONTENTS

INTRODUCTION:
We're recovering people-pleasers - Is that okay with you?

PART 1:
SELF-AWARENESS

CHAPTER 1:
What is people-pleasing?

CHAPTER 2:
Why do we people-please?

PART 2:
SELF-COMPASSION

CHAPTER 3:
Why do I people-please?

CHAPTER 4:
How do I stop people-pleasing?

PART 3:
SELF-CARE

CHAPTER 5:
How do I please myself?

CHAPTER 6:
How do I thrive in my relationships?

CONCLUSION:
Where do we go from here?

BREAKING UP WITH PEOPLE-PLEASING

By Aubree Henderson & Andrea Seydel

DEDICATION

*For those who always put themselves last –
you were made for more than keeping
other people comfortable.*

INTRODUCTION

We're recovering people-pleasers - Is that okay with you?

Maybe you have been told that people love you because you are willing to do anything to make them happy. Maybe people who are takers line up to date you. Even though you are busy, you may constantly get asked to be responsible for many things. You may find that saying no just leaves you feeling guilty or worse - worried you will not be liked, accepted, or loved. Maybe you believe that you are only worthy of love if you give everything to someone else, that if you love hard enough others will love you back in the same way. People-pleasing behaviour may leave you feeling frustrated, exhausted, and thinking you have zero time for yourself. As the authors of this book, and as recovering people-pleasers ourselves, we know how you feel. It feels great to be appreciated, loved, and accepted by others in our lives, but it can come with damaging effects. It can become exhausting, emotionally draining, and stressful keeping up with the demands of others. We know all too well the pain of people-pleasing. We are recovering (yes, still recovering!) people-pleasers. It is a work in progress, a journey to a healthier way of living - and we are here to show you the way. The good news is that it's not too late; you can take your life back.

People-pleasing may not seem or sound all that negative. After all, what could be wrong with making other people happy? While kindness and caring are admirable qualities (practicing kindness has even been shown to promote our well-being!) there is a difference between people-pleasing and just being extremely kind to others. People-pleasing generally goes beyond simple kindness. You probably picked up this book because you recognize that you might be going out of your way and giving up your time and energy to the point that it is no longer comfortable. You may also still be unsure whether you are a people-pleaser - don't worry! In this book, you will discover what people-pleasing is, if you are in fact a people-pleaser, how it might be negatively affecting you, and many powerful strategies to create boundaries, express your needs, and prevent burnout.

We both used to believe that being kind, agreeable, and accommodating would guarantee us to win the love and acceptance of others. We used to avoid conflict and difficult emotions to please others. We learned that some people were easy to please, while others drained the life right out of us. We both believed to our core that if we were nice enough to others they would love us back in the same manner and magnitude. All the while, we did not realize that we were afraid of being rejected, abandoned, or disliked. For each of us, it reached the point where our efforts to please others left us feeling depleted, empty, disrespected, and taken advantage of. You might be feeling the same - which is why you picked up this book! It became apparent in both of our individual lives that trying to please others - at times being successful, and other times failing - becomes depleting.

This book will share the lessons and strategies we have learned through years of trial and error. Within these pages you will find the tools, science, and resiliency skills you can use to finally break free from people-pleasing - the same practices that have been instrumental in our own healing journeys. Life can be more nourishing, meaningful, and sustainable when you stop the cycle and break up with people-pleasing once and for all.

Breaking up with people-pleasing can feel like an actual romantic breakup. It can be just as heartbreaking, emotional, and painful at times. It is also an excellent opportunity for self-discovery. It is easy to fall back into old patterns when we are in the discomfort that comes with growth, but we promise you that there is something better out there.

This process is a journey. We encourage you to be loving and supportive of yourself through this process. Sit back and be open to a more fulfilling new way of being, one that is empowering and full of self-awareness, self-compassion, and self-care.

In this book we will walk you through some key questions:

What is people-pleasing?
Why do we people-please?
Why do I people-please?
How do I stop people-pleasing?
How can I please myself?
How do I thrive in my relationships?

We are so excited to have you on this journey with us!

Let's get started.

PART 1: SELF-AWARENESS

CHAPTER 1: WHAT IS PEOPLE-PLEASING?

In this chapter, you will:

- Gain a clear understanding of people-pleasing.
- Be able to identify and recognize people-pleasing behaviour.
- Learn the difference between caring and people-pleasing.
- Recognize the harmful side effects of people-pleasing.
- Complete a self-assessment.

What is people-pleasing?

The desire to make others happy can be powerful. Saying yes to everything that is being asked of you in hopes of being accepted and liked by others can also be powerfully exhausting. Are you one of those "nice" people that is known for always being helpful and kind? Maybe you continuously strive for happy relationships and connection by routinely putting others' needs before your own. Guess what? You will never be able to be all things to all people. Have you ever wondered what is beneath this desire to please? Do you ever wish you could stop caring what people think and stop people-pleasing? People-pleasing *sounds* nice, but it can have long-term costs to your wellness and emotional health, and it may backfire on you at any moment.

- Do you feel pressure to say yes to everyone's requests of you?
- Are you afraid of conflict or inconveniencing others?
- Do you crave compliments and fear criticism?
- Do you frequently worry about what others think of you?
- Do you find yourself over-explaining your mistakes?
- Do you catch yourself frequently saying sorry?

If you answered *yes* to any of these questions, you might be a people-pleaser. Chances are good if the title of this book caught your attention, you are seeking help because you identify as a people-pleaser.

People-pleasing might not seem all that bad. After all, what could be wrong with the concept of being nice to other people? What is negative about trying to help others be happy? People-pleasing is much greater than simple acts of kindness. Think about it: if everyone in the world was demanding and imposing their will on everyone else in the world, it would be full of conflict and tension. Some degree of people-pleasing is essential. The problem arises when chronic people-pleasing behaviour causes you to lose your own path, personal happiness, and healthy self-worth along the way. People-pleasing involves changing and altering your own behaviours and life for the sake of another person's feelings and desires.

So, what exactly is people-pleasing? It might look like going out of your way to do things for people, based on what you think they need and want. You end up giving up your own time and energy to make others happy and better yet, make them like you more. A people-pleaser is someone who has an emotional need to please others, often at the expense of his or her own needs or desires.

According to Psychiatrist and Social Connection expert Samantha Boardman, "Being a *people-pleaser* isn't all bad. It shows that you are a caring person who values social connections and enjoys making others happy." People-pleasing isn't inherently negative, and these tendencies often come from a good place of caring and concern. Part of having relationships and connection with others involves taking their needs, wants, and feelings into consideration.

On the surface, it seems like you are helpful, extremely nice and super agreeable. But underneath, true people-pleasers might be struggling as they put others needs before their own, not thinking about themselves. People-pleasing is a very common challenge and may also be recognized as being the "nice girl" or "nice guy", codependency, anxious attachment, and being a doormat. These behaviours begin as a strategy to maintain connections and closeness with people who may be inconsistently available. A fear of abandonment and fear of rejection tends to be at the heart of people-pleasing.

If this feels like a lot to process, don't worry - this book will walk you through self-awareness, self-compassion, and self-care in a loving way that will transform your life. If you recognize yourself in this discussion, take heart. Knowing what contributes to people-pleasing behaviours and how it might be showing up negatively in your life is the first step towards empowerment. This first step is self-awareness without judgment, and then you can begin to gently change how you relate to yourself and to others. Let's first verify whether you're showing people-pleasing behaviours.

Are you a people-pleaser?

Here are common habits of people-pleasing - how many of these statements apply to you?

- You struggle with saying "no."
- People take advantage of your kindness and generosity.
- You become emotionally dependent in your relationships.
- You want to avoid bad feelings or conflict in relationships.
- You crave affirmation and approval from others.
- You act based on what you think other people want from you.
- You put yourself in other people's shoes often.
- You try to make everyone happy.
- Showing compassion towards yourself is challenging.
- You find it easy to see the good in others.
- You don't like feeling negative emotions.
- You are terrified of disappointing others.
- You assume the best about others, but not yourself.
- You find it hard to assert yourself.
- You find self-worth outside of yourself.
- You find it hard to recognize how you really feel.
- You suppress a lot of emotion.
- You fear not belonging and want to fit in.

- You're so busy helping others, don't have any free time.
- You take pride in sacrificing your own needs.
- You are quick to agree with others' opinions, even when you don't actually agree.
- You have a fear of rejection or not being liked.
- You feel guilty when you say "no."
- You hold back your own opinions.
- You find yourself feeling frustrated and resentful in your relationships.
- Arguments and conflict upset you a great deal.
- Doing things for others makes you feel worthy or useful.
- You give freely, and feel shocked when you don't get something in return.
- You find it hard to be your true self.
- You fear disappointing others.
- You feel pressure to keep up the appearance of happiness and success.
- You often feel stressed, burned out, and exhausted.
- You have a hard time setting boundaries.
- You feel shattered and broken when someone criticizes you.

REFLECTION EXERCISE:

Do you identify with this list? How many of these people-pleasing behaviours do you recognize in your own life? Simply observe and notice without judgment.

_____

_____

_____

_____

_____

What people-pleasing might look like:

People-pleasing shows up in many different ways.

You might have a tendency to agree with others' opinions or ideas, even when you disagree, in order to be liked or accepted. You may catch yourself apologizing often, as you fear that others may not be happy with you or worry what they might be thinking. You may also notice that it is hard for you to say no to people when they ask you to do something - you simply don't want to let them down. It may feel uncomfortable for you if someone is angry with you or has a difference of opinion. You may go to great lengths in order to avoid conflict, struggling to stand up for your own values. You may also neglect your own needs, wants, and desires in order to please someone else.

Over time, this neglect ends up making you feel resentful and exhausted. Exhaustion also comes from not being able to say "no" or set boundaries. As a result, you may find it hard to actually follow through on things that you have said yes to, as you have overbooked and overburdened yourself with obligations. You may find your schedule is booked and filled with activities that you believe other people want you to do, not necessarily things that *you* want to do.

You may not like how it feels when you disappoint someone. You may often feel that people will get upset with you if you don't measure up. It's hard to think of the thought of someone being displeased by you, so you do what it takes to make them happy and please them. You will often feel resentful when you feel someone isn't returning the same level of kindness. When you do get into an argument or any type of conflict, you become very upset. When someone criticizes you, you feel shattered and broken. You may also find it hard to stand up for yourself or speak up about your true feelings when you are hurt. It may be hard to express your discontent or negative emotions toward others. You may even find yourself apologizing often as you fear other people might blame you for something. You likely experience excessive guilt and anxiety when you can't satisfy others' needs or desires - the last thing that you want is to have people disapprove of or be disappointed in you.

You enjoy doing things for other people. Doing things for others makes you feel a sense of worthiness and makes you feel useful. You often find yourself trying to help others. You would define yourself as a giver. Helping others gives you a sense of self-worth and meaning in your life. You feel needed when you are helping someone else. Your world often becomes obsessed or preoccupied with the caring of others, so much so that you put your own needs aside. Caring for and pleasing others makes you feel a sense of control in your life.

REFLECTION EXERCISE:

Which people-pleasing behaviours are showing up in your life? Are they helping or hindering you? What purpose are they serving? Simply observe and notice without judgment.

_____
_____
_____
_____
_____

The Potential Downsides of Being a People-Pleaser:

At first, many people take the title of people-pleasing as a compliment, thinking:

Yeah, I'm a people-pleaser. What's wrong with that?
What's wrong with making others comfortable and taken care of?
Who doesn't love a people-pleaser?

Many people-pleasers confuse people-pleasing with caring and kindness. But people-pleasing can be a problem. But as we have learned, there is a difference between caring and people-pleasing. Let's take a look at healthy vs. unhealthy people-pleasing behaviours and how to recognize the negative side effects.

When you start to addictively put the needs of others before your own, there are going to be repercussions. It is common to want others to be happy, and we want them to be happy *with* us. People-pleasers often want to do things that will earn praise and please the important people in your life - this is normal human behaviour, especially in early life. But people-pleasing can quickly become problematic when you continuously put the needs of others before your own. People-pleasing is when you take the "good person" role to an excessive degree. Let's investigate the hidden dangers of chronic people-pleasing.

Here are some common consequences of people-pleasing:

- Taking on too many responsibilities.
- Caving to pressures and demands from others.
- Holding yourself back from your true greatness.
- Harboring buried resentments.
- Lack of individual identity.
- Difficulty being your authentic self.
- Mental and emotional exhaustion.
- Poor time management.
- Isolation or disconnection in relationships.
- Friends that take advantage of you.
- Being a target of manipulation.
- Making promises you can't keep.
- Feeling guilt and shame.
- Feeling overlooked.
- Rarely prioritizing self-care.
- Having no time for yourself.
- Doing things you don't really want to be doing.
- Feeling stress and pressure to be all things to all people.

As psychologist Harriet Braiker says, "To please is a disease, and in excess, it can become an addiction that eventually results in you neglecting your own needs and wants, and ironically losing the respect of the people you are trying to please." (Braiker 2001).

Awareness and acceptance are the first steps towards shifting away from unhealthy behaviours. As recovering people-pleasers ourselves, we know firsthand about how difficult it can be to be this person - and we want to assure you that it is possible to curb people-pleasing behaviour and still be a kind person!

Not only does people-pleasing affect your mental health, it is also emotionally draining. It begins to wear on your energy and your resilience. In addition to this exhaustion and depletion, the shadow side of people-pleasing is the resentment it creates towards others who do not reciprocate your kindness. People-pleasing also affects the quality of your relationships, including your relationship with yourself. At the heart of people-pleasing is the belief that we are not enough, and we need to prove our worthiness with validation from others. This drives us to be useful, selfless, nurturing, and helpful to others in order to gain the love and acceptance we are unable to source from within.

People-pleasers have a tendency to put themselves at the bottom of their own priority list. They struggle with setting limits or saying no, even when they're already at their capacity of things to do. They find it hard to speak up and communicate their own needs or even ask for help for fear that it may inconvenience someone else.

Let us be clear: wanting to take care of others and be kind is a beautiful approach to life. Your heart is in the right place. However, people-pleasing is ultimately doing harm if it's at the expense of your own wellbeing.

If you identify as a people-pleaser, looking directly at the shadows of these patterns of behaviour can feel uncomfortable. Take a breath - the good news is that you have what it takes to do the inner work and build healthier habits. In the coming pages, you will discover how to break free from the exhaustion, overwhelm, and disappointment of people-pleasing.

REFLECTION EXERCISE:

What are the shadow sides of people-pleasing for you? How does it make you feel? Where does it show up in your life? Simply observe and notice without judgment.

_____

_____

_____

_____

_____

The Close Family of People-Pleasing:

This book dives deep into people-pleasing, but as we explore this phenomenon it may also be helpful to understand some related concepts in the family of people-pleasing.

Codependent, caretaker, enabler, doormat, pushover, and control freak are all close cousins to the people-pleaser. The general definition of people-pleasing we have used in this book is anyone that puts other people's needs ahead of their own on a consistent basis. Codependency occurs when you are a people-pleaser who will go to virtually any lengths to avoid unpleasant conflict with others. In Melody Beattie's book *Codependent No More*, she defines a codependent person as: "One who has let another person's behaviour affect him or her, and who is obsessed with controlling that person's behaviour through their actions and desire to limit conflict" (Beattie 1992). It means that making choices that solely please others (or try to control them) while those decisions and behaviours end up impacting their own lives. Sometimes labelled as a doormat, all the needs of others become the priority of the people-pleaser. Breaking free from codependency is to learn that you and your needs matter, too. Codependency can lead to obsessive and controlling behaviours, which can end up consuming your life. You often find it hard to say no or set limits, and as a result people take advantage of you. People who identify as codependent usually play the role of the "rescuer" in a relationship with someone who is impaired or ill in some way. You are constantly trying to help, fix, people-please, change, or rescue. Codependents derive self-worth from helping and pleasing others. Caretaking becomes your identity as you become wrapped up in your partner, to the point that you lose yourself in the process. Codependency is characterized by a person belonging to a one-sided relationship where one person relies on the other for meeting nearly all of their emotional needs. The term enabler generally describes someone whose behaviour allows another to continue by "helping," leading to self-destructive patterns of behaviour. Do you expend all of your energy in meeting your partner's needs? Are you the one that makes sacrifices in your relationship? Then you may be in a codependent relationship. Codependency and people-pleasing are in the same family. Think of people-pleasing as a symptom of being in a codependent relationship.

Identifying as a people-pleaser does not necessarily mean you are also codependent, an enabler, rescuer, or pushover - but understanding the "family" of people-pleasing behaviours and related phenomena can help us to better understand ourselves and our own patterns to help us move forward toward a healthier future.

CHAPTER 1 KEY TAKEAWAYS:

- A people-pleaser is someone who has a compulsive need to please others.
- Being a people-pleaser isn't all bad, but it can have harmful side effects.
- People-pleasing has many symptoms - it can look like being unable to say no, over apologizing, or neglecting one's own needs.
- People-pleasers often neglect or disregard their own needs to prioritize the needs of others, leading to exhaustion and resentment.

CHAPTER 2: WHY DO WE PEOPLE-PLEASE?

Now that we've defined what people-pleasing is and what it might look like, we'll dig into what may be the most important piece to understand: Why?

Why do we people-please?
Why does people-pleasing happen?
Why do we continue to do it if we know it's harmful and limiting us in our relationships?

In this chapter, you will:

- Discover some common reasons why humans engage in people-pleasing behaviour.
- Uncover the roots, patterns, and stories that contribute to people-pleasing.
- Understand the needs that people-pleasing could be fulfilling.

Why did you become a people-pleaser? The stories you might be telling yourself:

Each of us is unique with our own stories, identities, and relational experiences that will inform and influence our personal experiences with people-pleasing. But even with that important caveat, there are a few primary reasons *we*, as humans broadly, engage in people-pleasing behaviour.

The first is that we give love, care, and support with an implicit expectation of reciprocating.

You might find the internal voice that says:

"If I can help others be happy and solve their problems, surely I will find the love and acceptance I've been missing."

Often, love, care, and support are given with the hidden desire for others to treat us in the same manner.

There are many people-pleasers out there who might deny this or feel defensive about it initially. Maybe that's you right now. You might read this and think, "No, I'm giving selflessly. I just love helping people - and I love helping because it's the right thing to do! I don't like to say no or set boundaries because I just have so much love to give." Sound familiar? It did for us, too. As recovering people-pleasers, we know that this is just a story we tell ourselves. It can be a challenging concept to accept - stay with us.

Remember - this book is written by two people who have experienced all the effects of people-pleasing and are recovering. You are not alone. At points in our journeys, we believed that we were simply giving to others selflessly without ulterior motives. Meanwhile, we were continually burning ourselves out from caretaking, neglecting boundaries, and letting people walk all over us. When we found ourselves being overly helpful, caring, and nurturing to others, we were (whether consciously or unconsciously) trying to earn that same type of care for ourselves in return.

You may be reading this and feeling that it doesn't apply to you, because you're a naturally giving and nurturing person. We don't disagree with you! But often, people-pleasing behaviour can have a manipulative or controlling undercurrent, whether you are aware of it or not. The motivation to engage in these people-pleasing behaviours is the desire for someone to *reciprocate* your level of care. You may hope that if you are demonstrative enough in your care and keep showing up for others, they will take the hint and show you that same care in return.

If you're reading this and you're feeling defensive, or if you're thinking, "Ok, sure, maybe some people do this - but this isn't me," take a moment to stop and reflect. We are asking you to take an honest look at the "why" behind your people-pleasing. Do you wish that people reciprocated your care? Or do you find yourself shocked by others' lack of caregiving and support?

Here is another way to look at this concept. What if you were told definitively, and with absolute certainty, that no one was ever going to reciprocate your gestures of caring? What if you were told that no matter how much you learn to anticipate someone else's needs, no matter how many gifts you give, and no matter how many times you show up for someone when they need you, that they would not do the same for you? What if no matter how many times you neglect your own needs for someone else, no matter how many times you decide your own life based on what someone else wants, they will never, EVER do the same for you?

What if you were told that no one is going to rise to that occasion and show up for you the way you're showing up for them? How does that sit with you? How does that feel?

Do you still feel just as motivated to keep trying until someone finally treats you as well as you've treated them? Do you think that if you can just care hard enough, you can change someone into the type of person who can love you?

Remember, there is no judgment here. We understand and are on a lifelong people-pleasing recovery journey with you. These patterns and stories are widespread amongst people-pleasers. If you had told us at the height of our people-pleasing that our behaviours were a strategy to get our own needs met, we probably wouldn't have believed you! We know exactly how it feels to have this revelation. Recognizing this is a crucial step in moving forward toward healthier relationships!

For anyone wondering, "How on earth is helping others a BAD thing?!" know that it is okay to get genuine joy out of doing kind or encouraging things for others or helping to make their lives easier. Support and kindness alone are not negative or harmful qualities! The key is to really interrogate and understand your motivations: WHY are you doing these things? It is a simple question you can become aware of on a regular basis. Think about why you are supporting and being kind to others. Is it out of generosity, or because you are hoping they will reciprocate?

Next time you find yourself going out of your way to meet someone else's needs, try asking yourself these questions:

- Am I doing this because I hope this person will do the same for me?
- Am I trying to convince this person that they need me?
- Am I trying to love this person enough that they love me back the way I want to be loved?

If the answer to any of these questions is yes, take a moment to ask yourself:

- What is stopping me from asking for what I want or need directly?
- What would it look like to name my needs for the other person, giving them the chance to respond?

Notice the thoughts and feelings that come up as you ask yourself these questions. Maybe the idea of asking for what you need directly brings up anxiety, discomfort, or fear. That's ok! Dig more deeply into that. What is the fear that causes you to try to get your needs met by people-pleasing, rather than getting your needs met by asking for what you need? We recommend printing these powerful questions and put them somewhere where you will see them often.

The roots, patterns, and stories that contribute to people-pleasing:

Another reason why people engage in people-pleasing behaviour - and this one is broader than our relationships with others - is the idea that people-pleasing is genuinely central to our identity or our perceived role in the world. People-pleasing becomes the way that we source our worth. It's how we feel helpful and how we feel connected to the people around us. It is the internal voice that says:

"If I don't make others happy or make their lives easier, then my life has no purpose."

It can apply more broadly to your role as a human in the world and on a more micro level to your role in a particular relationship. We begin to believe that if we stop people-pleasing, then a particular person (or people in general) might not want to be in a relationship with us anymore. You can see how important people-pleasing might become if this is our belief - that they might be keeping us around simply because we are helpful or useful or make them feel good. As a result, our identity as a people-pleaser becomes central to maintaining that relationship. We often fear that changing the behaviour might jeopardize that relationship. It could be true with a partner, with friends, with family, or anyone in our life who matters to us. When we show up in any role for a long time, it can feel like we don't know who we are anymore when we're not playing that role. You can see how this might affect who we are and how we feel worthy.

A result of this thinking is that we begin to believe that our ability to make another person happy, to be flexible and accommodating, or to solve their problems for them - the people-pleasing behaviour - is somehow the only thing we have to offer in a relationship. This belief makes us doubt or question ourselves and our identity.

If you struggle with this belief, please hear us when we tell you: you have so much more to offer others than keeping them comfortable or offering convenience. Take time to ask yourself what value you'd bring to the relationship if you weren't focused on making that other person happy and ensuring they have what they need.

It is critical that we interrogate this belief, because left unchallenged, it will have you questioning your very worth and value as a human being. It can be hard to take an honest look at your value. Because we overemphasize our people-pleasing as our only value-add in relationships, many of us struggle to tune in to what it is that we want or need in our lives and what makes us truly feel alive. This means it is essential that you make an active effort to reconnect with your desires as you heal from people-pleasing.

The reason we use the word "reconnect" as opposed to just prioritizing or following your desires is that after you've engaged in people-pleasing behaviour or codependency for a long time, you will begin to get disconnected from what you need. It will require an active and intentional process to get reconnected to what you need and want for yourself.

Understanding what you want and need is at the very core of who you are as a human. Many of us were taught to deprioritize our own needs in early life, and have spent years without really feeling connected to our essence and the things that bring us true joy and meaning. And without having that scaffolded and supported process of reconnection, the idea of letting go of people-pleasing can be terrifying and daunting - because it is one thing to decide: "I need to stop being such a people-pleaser and really please myself and focus on what I want" - but it can be a genuinely terrifying realization when you have to ask yourself, "Oh no, wait - what do I want?!"

People-pleasing becomes so central to our identity that it becomes scary to let go - because we forget who we are underneath it. We are so busy prioritizing others' needs that we completely lose sight of our own.

The needs that people-pleasing could be fulfilling:

Not everyone is comfortable evaluating their own needs. The final "why" behind people-pleasing that we'll cover in this chapter is that people-pleasing serves as a distraction from our own painful emotions.

It is the inner voice that says:

"Focusing on other people's problems means I can avoid looking at my own."

Statements like this are a common experience for people-pleasers and one we don't talk about enough. And, of course we don't - because we tend to think of people-pleasers as entirely focused on others! The idea of our own pain, our own needs, and our own growth areas are naturally de-centered, and for many people-pleasers, that feels much more comfortable than the experience of looking within and staring our pain right in the face.

This avoidance makes sense from an evolutionary perspective; wanting to avoid pain is adaptive! So many of our behaviours - whether that's our impulse to people-please, the ways we want to meet others' needs, how we want to feel needed by someone - are driven by an *avoidance* of painful emotion.

When we are people-pleasing, we focus primarily on what other people are going through, often leaning in and trying to solve *their* problems. We are doing whatever we can to keep them from getting upset, hurt, or offended. We are making sure we are making choices that will keep *them* comfortable. What we aren't as conscious of though, is that by immersing ourselves in someone else's (or several someone else's) emotional experiences, we create a kind of escape from our own emotions, and that includes our own pain.

If you are unsure about whether your people-pleasing is driven by avoidance of painful emotion, ask yourself these questions:

- Which painful feelings am I avoiding by overidentifying with the feelings of others?
- What emotional pain do I get to ignore when I focus all my energy on keeping someone else happy?
- What feelings come up for me that I dismiss as "not a big deal?"
- What is the feeling or type of pain that I will avoid at all costs?

Remember that this is a method of self-protection. We think, "Oh, how convenient - I get to skip over the part where I hurt, *and* someone else can feel better! It's a win-win!"

Unfortunately, what happens is that when you spend your emotional energy attending exclusively to others the pain you're trying to suppress WILL reappear, and you'll have spent all of your emotional energy on holding someone else's. You will leave yourself without the emotional resources to cope with your own needs effectively.

The answer is not to ignore other people's pain completely and somehow become entirely self-centered. That is not the antidote to people-pleasing. If it was, you wouldn't have picked up this book.

We can't ignore our inner world of emotion by throwing ourselves into someone else's. A balanced approach ultimately requires that you regularly reflect on and confront your own emotional experiences, your pain, and your triggers. When you find yourself drawn to trying to resolve someone else's pain, fix someone else's problem, or get hyper-involved with someone else's emotions, a healthy approach requires that you are taking that intentional pause to ask yourself, "What am I avoiding looking at within myself by over-identifying with this other person? What is the pain or the emotion that I'm avoiding within myself? How can I make separate space to address that?"

The "why" behind people-pleasing - the reasons we engage in people-pleasing patterns:

- We people-please because we think it will help fulfill our emotional needs.

- People-pleasing becomes central to our identity, and we lose sight of who we are outside people-pleasing.

- People-pleasing allows us to avoid looking at our own pain by letting us fixate on other people's pain instead.

Understanding the motivation behind any of our behaviours is deeply important, especially in areas where we are pursuing growth or change. We must understand the root of the behaviour, and the need it's meeting for us. With people-pleasing, we can convince ourselves that these tendencies meet our need for love and affection, our need for identity and role in the world and in our relationships, and our need for a way to cope with pain.

The problem, however, is that people-pleasing is not fully meeting any of these needs. People-pleasing leaves us feeling unfulfilled and unsatisfied - and that's why we're breaking up with it. That's why you picked up this book! You aren't getting what you need from people-pleasing, and you know there has got to be a better way.

REFLECTION EXERCISE:

Which of these three "why"s of people-pleasing do you identify most with?

How did you feel reading this chapter?

Did you recognize yourself in any of these examples?

What is a new question you'll ask yourself to uncover your motivations for people-pleasing behaviour?

_____
_____
_____
_____
_____

CHAPTER 2 KEY TAKEAWAYS:

- People-pleasing is a response to stories that we tell ourselves about our worth and role in relationships.
- Understanding the "why" underneath our people-pleasing behaviour is key to deconstructing this behaviour and developing healthier habits moving forward.

PART 2: SELF-COMPASSION

CHAPTER 3:
WHY DO I PEOPLE-PLEASE?

In the previous chapter, we talked about why *we* (as a human collective) people-please - the three big "why"s behind people-pleasing as a phenomenon.

In this chapter, you will go even deeper and get more personal. You will learn strategies to uncover and unearth your personal *why* for the ways that people-pleasing or codependency might show up for you.

In this chapter, you will:

- Outline a strategy to uncover the fear that drives your people-pleasing behaviour.
- Identify the core beliefs about yourself that contribute to people-pleasing.
- Understand where our core beliefs and fears come from and how to approach them.

We have already reviewed some common reasons why we engage in people-pleasing behaviour. These broader and more global learnings become most helpful and applicable when we apply them to our own lives. It is the moment when we recognize as individuals: "I'm a people-pleaser. I know I am. I want to stop, but I don't know how. I don't know any other way to relate to people - but I know that I don't want to do this anymore."

Naturally, the first question we use to explore is "why?" and for most people, the more significant "why" for their people-pleasing is going to fall into one of those three categories we talked about in the last chapter:

- We people-please because we think it will help fulfill our emotional needs.
- People-pleasing becomes central to our identity, and we lose sight of who we are outside people-pleasing.
- People-pleasing allows us to avoid looking at our own pain by letting us fixate on other people's pain instead.

You likely relate to one or more of these statements. Knowing our broader "why" gives us a little bit of insight and more clues about what's going on for you, and what overall need that people-pleasing is fulfilling for you - but it doesn't paint your whole picture. It doesn't tell us why you, as an individual, continue to engage with people-pleasing.

For example, let's say you relate deeply to the first statement: People-pleasing helps me fulfill an emotional need. Excellent - this is a valuable thing to know and a wonderful place to start! Knowing this information about yourself will help when you start to slip into a pattern of people-pleasing:

- When you find that you're saying yes to things when you want to say no.
- When you're not making your needs known.
- When you're letting things slide that violate your values because you're afraid to make others upset.

There doesn't have to be that helpless feeling of "I know this hurts me... why on earth am I doing it?!" because you know now that this is a way of getting an emotional need met for yourself. It is essentially the validation of recognizing, "Ok, I'm doing this for a reason. This is meeting some emotional need for me."

What this knowledge doesn't do, though, is help you see the very individualized and personal patterns you're playing out, or the specific emotional gaps you're trying to fill within yourself. It only shows you the broad "why" behind the issue - not the root for you as an individual.

Here is a truth that will help transform you on your healing journey: most things we perceive as being "wrong" or "flawed" or "broken" about ourselves - the patterns or habits we have developed and are trying to break - were created initially as survival mechanisms in childhood. Even if they do not serve us now, they are behaviours we learned early in life to keep ourselves alive and thriving. It benefits us to approach these traits and behaviours with compassion, because they developed for a reason and served us at one point in time. We developed those coping mechanisms to deal with unmet needs and help us survive our early life.

Of course, these habits express themselves in a painful or unhelpful way in adulthood, and we want to let them go. But it's crucial that we begin that process from a place of tenderness and compassion for why they developed in the first place if we ever hope to untangle ourselves from them.

With that in mind, we can begin by viewing our people-pleasing behaviour through a very compassionate lens, without judgment. We can take this line of questioning a layer deeper. You can say to yourself, "Ok, I know I'm people-pleasing as a way of having my emotional needs met. That feels right to me. I think people are more likely to meet my emotional needs if I'm low-maintenance or easygoing, or go along with whatever they want."

The next step is then to ask yourself one critical question:

What is the fear underneath this behaviour?

Put a different way - What am I afraid will happen if I stop people-pleasing?

Now, we'd never ask anyone to simply quit a pervasive pattern or set of habits like people-pleasing cold-turkey. This approach not only sets people up to fail and is unrealistic - it can also be really scary and overwhelming!

Just as a thought exercise, imagine for a moment that we asked you to stop people-pleasing right now.

Depending on what that looks like for you - this could mean that I'm asking you:

- To say no when you mean no.
- To speak up when something makes you uncomfortable.
- To set clear and direct boundaries and limits in your relationships.
- To assert your own needs and ask for what you want explicitly.

Imagine that we asked you to start doing all of that right now, this second.

If you self-identify as a people-pleaser or as codependent, you probably feel uneasy about this idea. Why?

What are you afraid will happen?

Take a moment and think about this. At the end of this chapter, you'll do a written reflection exercise to help you process this further.

Remember, this is a helpful thought exercise for any pattern you're engaging in your relationships or how you show up in your life. It's essential to unpack the fears underneath any habit that you feel uncomfortable or afraid to let go of. It's not just for people-pleasers! If you're having trouble changing the way you show up or building new habits if you doubt whether you can do it - this is a helpful question.

What are you afraid will happen?

As you reflect on this, here are some common answers to this question that may jog your thinking:

- I'm afraid I'll say no when I want to say no, and they'll make me do it anyway.
- I'm afraid I'll ask for what I need, and they'll laugh at me.
- I'm worried that if I can't make other people happy and comfortable, I'm not worth anything.
- I'm so scared that if I'm not helping other people with their problems, I'll have to sit on my own, and I won't be able to solve them.

Identify the core beliefs about yourself that contribute to people-pleasing:

The answer to the question: "What is the fear underneath my people-pleasing?" is often informed by actual realities from our personal history and experiences.

If you've shared your feelings or perspective and been rejected for it, it makes sense that you'd then feel afraid of rejection and avoid it at all costs. You would likely adapt to prevent rejection because rejection is painful.

If you've had your needs overpowered or undermined by someone else despite making those needs known, you're a hell of a lot less likely to think it's necessary or worth it to name your needs and your preferences.

Your answer to this question, figuring out not only the "why" but also what the fear is for you, reveals more of the specifics of what's underneath this behaviour. It helps you get more information about the specific types of painful emotional experiences you are trying to avoid and where you're using people-pleasing as a band-aid to that problem.

These examples are also powerful because, most of the time, people-pleasing is not filling that gap.

It's not meeting that emotional need.
It's not cancelling out *your* pain just because you're focused on someone else's.
It's not providing you with a meaningful identity.

It might be helping you avoid the pain of rejection or control as you've known it previously - but if you're honest with yourself, you know that you can't numb out or avoid pain without numbing everything else as well.

It is where the most complex truth of all comes in:

If you are a people-pleaser, you are living inauthentically.

Let's say that again.

If you are a people-pleaser and are actively engaging in people-pleasing behaviour and patterns you are not living authentically.

You may be avoiding direct rejection by not stating what you need.

You may be avoiding someone directly disrespecting your needs and disregarding what you want even though you told them.

But in doing all of this, you are projecting a false version of yourself This means that even if the actual, authentic, *real* version of you isn't being rejected, it's not because you are being accepted or affirmed or that you truly belong - it's because your truth isn't even being seen.

Even if you are bypassing the experience of someone else rejecting you… *you* are still rejecting you. You are controlling yourself. You're fulfilling your own prophecy. And in a backwards kind of way, you're ensuring that the painful experiences you fear come to fruition. That's what's so painful about people-pleasing; as people-pleasers, what we want more than anything is to be known and seen and taken care of. Yet what we are guaranteeing is that our needs remain hidden, and our true selves go unseen. We are sabotaging what we long for the most.

These are not easy truths to hear. But we share them because we believe that understanding these truths is the only way to move forward to a more healthy and whole way of being. It is why we want to push you on this - because your underlying motivations and needs are the pieces of the puzzle that you must figure out before you can move forward in shifting your people-pleasing behaviour. You must be clear on the fears and motivations because that clarity is the only way to see that people-pleasing will not protect you from those fears.

Understanding this is your first step toward getting free.

Understand where our core beliefs and fears come from and how to approach them:

To get deeply acquainted with our fears, we first have to get friendly with that fear and see it for what it is. It's not your adult self being silly, or choosing to feel less-than or resentful in your relationships. These fears often originate in childhood. We're talking about you as a child or a young adult, the version of you who has a deep and pervasive wound. This could be a rejection wound, a power and control wound, or identity - something profoundly hurtful that you've created behavioural workarounds to avoid. These are ways that we package ourselves strategically and move through the world to protect that wound so it won't get bumped or reopened.

When we eventually decide we're ready to meet the world more freely, and not be burdened by our wounds and have our every move calculated so we don't disturb the wounds, we have to look at it. We have to inspect the damage carefully and gently and with genuine curiosity - because we have no hope of meaningfully changing these patterns if we don't look closely at where they're coming from.

So when you think about the patterns or habits you want to change but are having a hard time letting go of, ask yourself:

What is the fear here?

What am I afraid will happen if I stop showing up in this way?

We recommend taking the time to do some written reflection on these questions, and we've included space at the end of this chapter for just that. It can also help to visualize yourself in that hypothetical scenario and naming the fear not only in words, thoughts, and feelings but also in the sensations it brings up in your physical body.

Remember that there is no wrong way to do this exercise. What you are doing here is some inner exploration. You are digging into the beliefs, feelings, and fears underneath your habits, because over time those have become more and more subconscious and you want to bring them to the surface so you can be conscious and aware of them. This awareness will prepare you to shift those behaviours, which we'll start in the chapters ahead.

REFLECTION EXERCISE:

What are you afraid will happen if you stop people-pleasing?

When you think about changing the way you show up, what fear emerges?

What is the worst-case scenario?

When you consider this, what do you feel in your physical body?

_____
_____
_____
_____
_____

CHAPTER 3 KEY TAKEAWAYS:

- People-pleasing is a fear response – a behaviour that develops to avoid a feared outcome.
- When you identify the fear underlying your people-pleasing behaviour, you get to the root of the issue and can understand and soothe that fear with new, healthier responses instead of people-pleasing.

CHAPTER 4: HOW DO I STOP PEOPLE-PLEASING?

In the last chapter, you went deep and got more personal. You learned strategies to uncover and unearth your personal "WHY" for the ways that people-pleasing or codependency might be showing up for you. This section will discover how to confront people-pleasing head-on while also learning how to engage with negative emotions safely. We will discuss practices for self-acceptance, techniques for new beliefs, and how to rewire your brain and thinking.

In this section, you will:

- Learn to confront people-pleasing.
- Learn to engage with negative emotions safely.
- Discover practices for self-acceptance.
- Create new beliefs.
- Learn to rewire your brain and thinking.

Break up with people-pleasing (but still be kind): How do I stop people-pleasing?

The best way out of people-pleasing is to become more aware of your inner world and do so in a compassionate manner. How do you stop people-pleasing and start living your life in a way that is on your terms? In this section, you will discover the power of self-awareness and taking the time to look at your thoughts and feelings. You have the opportunity to learn and grow from gaining self-awareness combined with self-compassion. You have already come to a point in your life that you realize doing too much and being all things to all people is not sustainable or healthy for you. Learning techniques for increasing self-awareness and self-acceptance is a significant part of the process for breaking up with people-pleasing. This is an evolving process that will not happen overnight. This process is about you and your ability to find ways to change your responses to people and finally live your life on your terms.

Learn how to confront people-pleasing:

Why am I constantly seeking validation?
How can I stop being a people-pleaser?
Why do I feel like people don't like me or worry about what they think?

You have found some of the answers to these questions from the previous section as to why you people-please, and this knowledge will be essential to grow and move forward. You have already established that you are a people-pleaser. You know some of the reasons that you might be people-pleasing. You are now at a point where you can learn how to confront the people-pleasing head-on. It is time for you to find your voice, learn to set your boundaries, and stop being a people-pleaser. This is a beautiful opportunity for you to take control of your own life!

The first step is to recognize and admit that people-pleasing is a choice. Gone are the days where you try so hard to make others happy and go out of your way to please others, even if it means taking your own valuable time and energy away from you. Gone are the days where you feel insecure and cannot speak up for your own needs and desires. You do not need to be a perfectionist or be all things to all people only to leave you feeling exhausted.

People-pleasing often seems so automatic that it can feel as though you don't have a choice - but with a bit of processing, planning, and preparation, you can take control and make major changes in your life.

How do you mentally choose to stop people-pleasing?

Self-awareness is the key to catching yourself in the habit of people-pleasing. Then, once you have a deeper understanding of when you people-please, understand why you are doing it. What might the rewards be for people-pleasing? Once you become more aware, you can then choose to start the process of change. In his book *The Power of Habit*, Charles Duhigg teaches us a whole new way of understanding human nature and its potential for transformation.

Duhigg shares that change might not be fast, and it isn't always easy - but with time and effort, almost any habit can be reshaped (Duhigg 2014). Duhigg's golden rules of habit change involve:

1. Keep an eye on what is driving the behaviour you want to change. In other words, what is driving you to people-please?

2. Identify what is reinforcing or rewarding the behaviour. What reward are you getting from people-pleasing?

3. Plan behaviour or another routine that will support that reward. What other behaviour can provide you with the same reward that people-pleasing has given you?

4. Identify the cues or situations that create the behaviour you want to change. What situations, with what people, or in what environments do you find yourself people-pleasing?

5. Choose a new routine with similar payoffs. What could you do instead of people-pleasing?

The bottom line in all this is that you have to choose - and plan - to change. According to Angela Duckworth, a University of Pennsylvania researcher, eventually you can turn self-discipline into a habit and design willpower habits to help you change your life and behaviours. The caveat, of course, is that you must deliberately intentionally design your habits, be consistent in practicing them, and make an active choice to change (Duckworth, Gendler, & Gross 2016).

REFLECTION EXERCISE:

List the situations and environments in which you find yourself people-pleasing.

What are the rewards that people-pleasing bring for you?

What behaviour do you want to replace? What is your new behaviour?

How can you build in a reward? How can you train your brain to expect rewards from the new behaviour?

List the ways you will be rewarded for not being people-pleasing.

_____
_____
_____
_____
_____

Actionable tips for breaking up with people-pleasing:

- List rewards of not people-pleasing.
- Catch yourself in the moment and notice when you are people-pleasing.
- Recognize that you have choices.
- Create a mantra or affirmation (ex: My needs matter, too.)
- Pause when in doubt, rather than automatically answering the way you think the other person wants you to
- Remember that other people's opinions are not more important than your own.
- Monitor your self-talk and whether you are being kind to yourself.
- Curb over apologizing by replacing "Sorry" with "Thank you".
- Be clear on your own goals and priorities.
- Create policies or personal rules (ex: I will not say "yes" automatically without giving myself time to think about my response.)
- Assert yourself and practice saying "no."

Learn to engage with negative emotions safely:

We all experience emotions, and as adults, sometimes it becomes challenging to navigate the rage of emotions you might encounter in a day. Your ability to feel and respond to your emotions impacts your physiological states and can even affect how you show up in your life. Sometimes it is challenging to work with negative emotions such as guilt, shame, rejection, fear, worry, or failure. Emotions are normal, human, and an essential part of life. Some emotions are positive, like happiness, pride, gratitude, excitement, and joy. Negative emotions such as sadness, guilt, jealousy, loneliness, rejection, or fear can be difficult and painful to navigate at times. However, negative emotions are impossible to avoid - from ourselves or others. People pleasers often struggle to tolerate negative emotions within ourselves or the individuals around us. Strengthening our capacity to process and respond to difficult emotions can help eliminate some of the fear & uncertainty that fuels people-pleasing.

Steps to process negative emotions:

Identify the emotion - Be aware of how you feel when you have negative emotions. Try to name what you're feeling. For example, "I feel rejected when I am left out." Know why you feel the way you do. Figure out what happened that got you to the point of this feeling. Be cautious of any impulse to blame others for your feelings & emotions - remember that you are able to recognize and explain your emotions without casting blame onto others. Accepting responsibility for your own emotional experience empowers you to respond to it more effectively. Be sure not to hide how you feel from yourself - accept that all emotions are natural and understandable. Try to refrain from judging yourself for having the emotions you feel or telling yourself you "should" feel something different. Observe these feelings and recognize them, non-judgmentally, for what they are. Mindfulness can be a space for practicing the habits of recognition and non-reactivity. Remember that self-awareness and non-reactivity are always available. Acknowledging how you feel is the first step towards safely engaging with your emotions.

Practice self-compassion - As people-pleasers, it can be easy to have compassion for others while truly struggling to have any compassion for yourself. In her book *Self-Compassion*, Kristin Neff teaches the power of positive self-talk and compassion as techniques to accept negative emotions as a natural part of the human experience. Offering compassion is about listening attentively to feelings, without judgement, and to remember that inherent goodness and worthiness remains even amid significant challenges (Neff 2011). This practice often comes easily to people-pleasers when it comes time to show compassion for others. On the other hand, self-compassion is more challenging because it can be challenging to see areas of suffering in your own life without judgment or shame. Self-compassion is like being your own best friend. According to Neff, the basic components of self-compassion are:

1. **Self-Kindness** - Self-kindness is the cessation of negative self-talk. It means that you've made an intentional choice to stop judging yourself for your suffering and practice kindness toward yourself and your own experience.
2. **Common Humanity** - We're all in this together and human. Remember that you are far from alone in experiencing feelings of shame and inadequacy. These hurdles make you human, everyone falls short sometimes, everyone makes mistakes, and everyone feels shame.
3. **Mindfulness** - Mindfulness is a powerful tool that helps you observe your feelings and the events of your life with calm and compassion. For instance, during a moment of difficulty, you might feel the urge to jump into action to avoid your true feelings. Mindfulness invites you to remain present in what you are feeling, rather than moving into action as an effort to avoid or bypass. Mindfulness techniques like deep breathing or meditation allow us to be present with our experiences and observe them rather than repress them.

Move into action - Once you have processed what you are feeling, you can then decide on ways to express your emotion. You may not need to express your emotion, and the acknowledgment is enough to make you feel better. But sometimes, you will want to take action to feel better.

Think about some of the ways you have expressed emotions in the past. Do you talk to friends, work out your emotions with a power walk, have a good cry, or journal? Rediscover your preferred ways to process what you are feeling. At the end of this chapter, you'll have a space to make a list of possible ways to express your emotions.

Another important way to actively process your emotion is to use positive emotion and gratitude to shift your mood. It can be easy to get stuck in a painful emotion, ruminating or dwelling on what's not going well. One helpful way to shift your mood is to focus on the good things in your life by practicing gratitude. You can use a gratitude practice to balance out the negative emotions with positive ones. Positive emotions don't just make us feel good, explains Barbara Fredrickson - they have the power to transform our minds, our bodies, and our ability to bounce back from hard times. Frederickson's research shows that a ratio of at least 3:1 - three positive emotions for every negative emotion - serves as a tipping point which helps determine how well we are able to flourish and bounce back from adversity (Fredrickson 2010). Building up your positive emotions creates a sense of happiness and wellbeing. Try to make it a habit to focus on and notice what is good by practicing gratitude, savouring the good, and mindfulness.

Physical movement can be a helpful way to move emotion through the body. Exercise can realize the stress that builds up with negative emotions and increase the feel-good neural chemicals. When you feel emotionally stuck, moving your body physically can help to shift that mindset.

Seek help. Finally, we would be remiss if we did not emphasize the importance of getting help from another person with complicated emotions that you are having trouble navigating on your own. For those of us who find it easy and natural to support others who are going through difficult times, we can forget that we deserve support and help as well. Find support from a group, life coach, professional, or trusted friend that can help you work through your emotions.

REFLECTION EXERCISE:

What negative emotions have you experienced lately? Name and acknowledge the emotion.

Why did you feel the way that you did?

What are possible ways you have or could express or process difficult emotions?

How do you change your mood?

Who can support you when processing negative emotions?

_____

_____

_____

_____

_____

Typical people-pleasing fears and how to break the pattern:

People-pleasers tend to have very similar fears:

- Fear of abandonment or rejection
- Fear of failure
- Fear of criticism and being disliked

People-pleasers also tend towards certain patterns of behaviour to avoid social stress or what is called cognitive dissonance. Cognitive dissonance describes the mental discomfort that results from holding two conflicting beliefs, values, or attitudes. People tend to seek consistency, and the conflict causes feelings of unease or discomfort.

People-pleasing is a type of cognitive dissonance. When you 'lie' to yourself or are not honouring who you truly are, you can experience an internal war. What you say or do disagrees with what you are thinking about or what you want. The discomfort that comes from these patterns can lead to stress, depression, or mental struggle. Many people-pleasing behaviours are simply ways of dealing with this cognitive dissonance. Let's look into these typical patterns of fear, why they are challenging, and how to break the habit.

Rid yourself of the fear of rejection. The fear of rejection and the shame associated with rejection is an underlying feeling that says "I have to do everything to make people happy or they might leave or stop caring about me." The fear of rejection is a powerful emotion that is very prevalent amongst people-pleasers. Sometimes the pain of rejection can be earth-shattering. The fear of rejection is real, and we often miss out on things because of it. According to cognitive-based therapies and the science of evolution, the fears of rejection are some of the deepest human fears. The brain is wired with the desire to belong and be a part of a group to survive. But have you ever stopped to consider what we are terrified of? As humans, we might be afraid that we are unlovable or will be alone. It is common also to carry a fear of pain and hurt. Being good and nice and seeking approval from others is a way to try and suppress the fear of rejection. Cultivating inner resilience by acknowledging and welcoming these emotions takes courage. As you become more confident and less afraid or intimidated by rejection, you become more empowered. Sometimes the desire to be liked is so strong, and the fear of rejection causes you to shut down, stop growing, or hold yourself back. The first step is to acknowledge that this fear is critical to our survival. The problem is when the fear of rejection is on overdrive. Most modern-day rejections will not impact our survival, so living with this fear becomes irrational and not healthy.

The best solution to the fears of rejection is to start working on accepting yourself. Some level of rejection is inevitable - the key to make peace with this is to embrace and accept your imperfections, shortcomings, flaws, and mistakes with compassion.

What is the narrative you are playing in your mind when someone does reject you? Chances are the narrative is mean, uncomfortable self-talk such as, "I am unworthy," "I'm unlovable." Self-love and self-acceptance become the key to processing the fear of rejection.

Rid yourself of the fear of failure. The fear of failure and the shame associated with loss is an underlying feeling that, "If I fail, I will disappoint people or be judged negatively." The fear of failure is an intense worry that you experience when you imagine all the horrible things if you fail to achieve your goal. The intense fear of failure increases the odds of holding you back or giving up. Ultimately, what makes us fearless is not the fact that we do not experience fear but that we are confident that we can deal with the consequences of our actions. Self-acceptance is the best way to overcome this fear of failure.

Rid yourself of the fear of criticism and being disliked. People-pleasers try to avoid conflict or any chance of upsetting others. It often involves backing down or going along with what others think or say. When fearing the upset of another human, the people-pleaser will hold back true feelings and try to keep the peace. Trying to keep the peace can be exhausting and cause the people-pleaser to lose themselves in the process. This harmony becomes false harmony as every healthy relationship has disagreements. This fear of being disliked and not approved or accepted creates unrealistic expectations along with the need to hide behind a mask of niceness. This tendency harbours resentment and cognitive dissonance. The only way out of this cycle is through self-acceptance.

Practices for self-acceptance:

- Acknowledge the possibility of positive outcomes, without becoming attached to them.
- Know that you are strong, and you can survive challenging situations and emotion.
- Look inward for validation, rather than looking only to others.
- Adopt a mantra or affirmation practice.
- Allow space for fear and uncertainty as an opportunity to grow and learn.
- Soothe yourself when feeling rejected.
- Be your own safe place.
- Affirm your value - "I am worthy."

- Practice loving yourself.
- Monitor your self-talk, and curb negative or unkind narratives while increasing positive self-talk.

REFLECTION EXERCISE:

Which of the common fears of people-pleasers resonate most for you?

How do these fears show up in your life?

Why do you think these fears show up?

How can you practice self-acceptance?

_____
_____
_____
_____
_____

Rewire your people-pleasing brain and thinking:

Most people-pleasers tend to seek out validation and appreciation from sources outside of themselves. Relying on validation from others means you gain confidence based purely on the external world - and that confidence can be taken away from you at any moment. To confront people-pleasing head-on, you must instead rely on internal validation, not external. In other words, if you are able to help yourself feel good, you don't need others to make you feel good. The question becomes, what makes you feel good? It is time to discover your ability for internal validation.

Your self-worth isn't based on what other people think of you. A deep and unshakeable sense of self-worth comes from nobody else but yourself, and requires you to recognize that you cannot please everybody. The only approval that you require is your own. You can't change what people think or feel, so it becomes clear that you don't need to waste your energy and time trying so hard to make others approve of you. Retraining your brain and creating new beliefs takes practice and time.

We can see the power of adopting a growth mindset when moving away from people-pleasing when we look at the work of Carol Dweck on mindset. Shifting from a fixed mindset - full of judgment and closed-off thinking - towards a growth mindset - full of learning and curiosity - supports your ability to break harmful habits like people-pleasing (Dweck 2006). Becoming your own best friend and adopting a mindset of opportunity, learning, and developing will open your world. People-pleasers tend to have a fixed mindset - a tendency to believe that you either have an ability or quality or you don't. Someone with a fixed mindset might say, "I am a people-pleaser. That's just who I am."

Adopting a growth mindset will allow you to tap into the power and ability to rewire your brain. A growth mindset is centered on the belief that one's innate skills, talents, and abilities can be developed and/or improved with determination. We can grow, change, and learn when we have a growth mindset. Neuroplasticity refers to the brains' ability to adapt and transform. Having a growth mindset that you can grow, learn, and remain curious is accepting the idea of neuroplasticity. If you believe you are malleable or adaptable, you are in a growth mindset, and believe that your mind can literally be changed.

The human brain is truly unique, and it can recover and reform itself. Internal validation rewiring is a form of what is called neuroplasticity. According to his book *The Science of Positive Brain Change*, neuroscientist Rick Hanson refers to neuroplasticity as the physiological changes in the brain that happen due to interaction with the environment. The connections among the cells in the brain reorganize in response to our changing needs. This dynamic process allows us to learn from and adapt to different experiences. Unlike a hardwired computer, the brain can receive updates over time. New pathways form, and others can fall dormant. We create new pathways or connections in our brains through repetition when we learn new things. As humans, we can encourage and stimulate these connections with our choices and actions. In other words, our minds change our brains to change our minds for the better (Hanson 2013).

It is exciting to learn that the brain can form new connections and pathways and these can change how our brains are wired. It is empowering to have this knowledge when we are trying to recover from people-pleasing (or any behaviour pattern, for that matter).

How to rewire your brain with a growth mindset and neuroplasticity:

Become conscious of negative thought patterns. Close your eyes and take a few deep breaths. Now bring your mind to a recent event where you were people-pleasing. Try to relive this moment in your mind. Can you identify the thought pattern behind this action? Ask yourself a series of "why" questions - why was I engaging in this behaviour? Why did I choose people-pleasing instead of naming my own needs? Listen to your answers consciously. Become familiar with your thought patterns. Become aware of the thought-emotion connection - every thought has an emotion that accompanies it. Increasing this awareness helps you understand the thought pattern better. Repeat the previous exercise, but this time focus on the feeling you had in your body. Where do you feel the sensations?

Change your questions, change your life. Marilee Adams talks about how we choose moment by moment to learn or to judge in her book *Change Your Questions, Change Your Life*. Through skillful questioning and question thinking, we can change our lives. Consider the questions, What's wrong? vs. What's right? Why am I such a failure? vs. What strengths can I draw on? Our questions determine our focus! Adams outlines the two basic paths we take in life, either the judger mindset path or the learner mindset path. A judger has automatic reactions, is blame-focused, and is win-lose relating. Conversely, a learner has thoughtful choices, is solution-focused, and is win-win relating (Adams 2009).

The costs of a judger mindset are tremendous. The enemy of good judgement is victimhood. Questions of a judger mindset might sound like: Why am I such a failure? Why bother? Why are they so stupid? Whose fault is this? A judger mindset is fundamental, critical, closed-minded, blaming, inflexible, limited, dismissive, rejecting, and defensive.

Conversely, in the learner mindset, the power is on! Questions might sound like: What happened? What do I want for myself? What can I learn? Learner mindset is accepting, responsible, comfortable, appreciative, solution-focused, flexible, adaptive, growth-oriented, accepting, collaborative, appreciative, resolving and sees unlimited possibilities. Remember - you have a choice! Moment to moment, you can choose curiosity to lead you to a learner mindset.

Stay mindful of your attention. Becoming aware of your feelings and the thoughts that create those feelings will help to loosen the grip and allow you to better deal with what is going on. Now that you have become conscious and aware of the pattern of people-pleasing, it will be much easier to catch yourself in this pattern. You can better respond to situations instead of reacting, using your awareness to focus your attention on small positive changes in your mindset. The more motivated we are for change, the more readily our brains will let go of negative thought patterns and replace them with empowering new ones. If you worry about letting someone down, for example, consciously refocus your mind to more positive, empowering thoughts.

You are not your brain. In his book *You Are Not Your Brain*, Jeffrey Schwartz breaks down deceptive brain messages. These messages are any false or inaccurate thought or any unhelpful or distracting impulse, urge, or desire that takes you away from your true goals and intentions in life (i.e., your true self). The good news is that you have an ally that can help you sculpt your brain to work for you, rather than against you: the mind. Repetitively thinking about something (including rumination, mental compulsions, and overthinking) or anything that you repeatedly do that is caused by a deceptive brain message takes you away from focusing on something beneficial. Helpful questions to increase your self-awareness include: How do you want to act? Who do you want to be? What are you doing that you want to stop? What are you currently *not* doing that you would like to do? (Schwartz & Gladding 2011)

Re-label, re-frame, re-focus, and re-value. Utilize these four strategies to work with your existing thought patterns:

- **Re-label** - Identify your deceptive brain messages and identify them as such - "This is a brain message that isn't true."
- **Re-frame** - Ask yourself why this thought bothers you. Change the perception of the importance of the misleading brain message. "Maybe this message isn't so important."
- **Re-focus** - Direct your attention towards a different activity or mental process that is productive or affirming.
- **Re-value** - See your thoughts, urges, and impulses for what they are simply thoughts, urges, and impulses.

New programming with affirmations. Affirmations can beautiful tools for reprogramming your mind. Once you catch and notice where you have recurring thoughts, emotions, and action, you can reprogram negative or unwanted thought patterns. You can start this programming with affirmations such as:

- I seek my own approval.
- I love myself.
- I am in control of my choices.
- It's ok for me to say no.
- My happiness is not dependent on others.

- It is not my job to make others happy.
- I am focusing on my self-care.
- Today, I am honouring my needs.

If you catch yourself moving to affirmations that are negative thoughts patterns, refocus and shift your attention away to make those connections weaker.

New programming with visualizations. Another form of programming is visualization or mental preplanning. Take the time to plan out responses and potential situations you may find yourself in during the day. Decide and practice how you would like to respond in these situations ahead of time. Visualize yourself in these potential situations. Practice visualizing yourself saying no with assertion.

New programming with implementation intention. This self-regulatory strategy, presented by social psychologist Peter Gollwitzer, is an effective tool to facilitate action and control in the future. It is simply a preplanned statement of "if …, then …" plans. It allows you to plan for potential obstacles that might get in the way of the desired action. An example might be, "if someone asks me to do something, then I will pause and say 'let me think about that and back to you.'" (Gollwitzer 1997)

Create new beliefs with self-talk. This is a powerful way to manage the words that you are saying to yourself. When you think and talk to yourself, your brain is listening and wiring. Be careful what you are saying to yourself, as your brain is listening. Shifting your self-talk towards being more positive, encouraging, and growth-mindset-oriented will enhance new programming in your brain. Stay mindful of the verbiage that you are using. Is it positive, or is it negative? Part of the rewiring is first being aware of negative self-talk and shifting it to more positive self-talk. For example, "I'm so mean to say no to that person." vs. "It's ok to say no, I am caring for myself, and I am important." Reassure yourself like you are your own best friend with positive suggestions and support. Silence the inner critic that criticizes and change the focus to soothing yourself. Stop negative, destructive thoughts in their tracks by recognizing and standing up to this inner voice. Positive self-talk can shift the doubting mind and disarm negative thoughts.

Build up your self-esteem with self-compassion. Building again on the work of Dr. Kristin Neff and self-compassion, we need to stop chasing self-esteem and start developing self-compassion. Throughout your life, you may find any number of reasons for criticizing yourself. It can be challenging to feel authentically good about yourself in a life filled with setbacks and despair. Consider the moments when you most often experience compassion in your life. Most people understand compassion primarily in terms of their relationships. Maybe you helped a close friend with marriage challenges or helped a daughter ashamed about her performance. Because these individuals are loved ones, you probably respond to their suffering with kindness. You listen attentively to their feelings, you don't judge them, and you assure them they're still good people even amid these challenges. It is how you show compassion for others. Self-compassion is harder to give than offering compassion to others. Harder to see areas of suffering in our own lives. So, the questions become: Where are you suffering? What are you needing? In Neff's book, *Self Compassion: The Proven Power of Being Kind to Yourself*, she describes the basic components of self-compassion as self-kindness, common humanity, and mindfulness (Neff 2011).

Self-kindness is the cessation of negative self-talk. It means making an intentional choice to stop judging yourself for your suffering. Step back from judgment impulses and seek to understand. Tell yourself, "I'm sorry you feel upset." During your next difficult moment, or if life is supposed to go a certain way and doesn't, tell yourself, "I'm sorry you feel upset," or, "Embarrassment is difficult." You might even hold yourself in a loving embrace so you can feel a physical sense of comfort. What can you do to give yourself some friendly comfort? When you show comfort to yourself, you're acknowledging your pain, but you're also playing the role of the caregiver to yourself.

Common humanity is the feeling that you are not alone. We are all in this together. Give yourself a break and permission to be human. Shame and inadequacy are extremely common. Life hurdles make you human. Permit yourself to be human by knowing everyone messes up, lets others down, and does things they regret. It means to forgive yourself when you realize or think that you've hurt someone. Just because you are feeling down doesn't mean that you are doing something wrong. It's ok not to be ok. Feel all your emotions and permit yourself to be happy, but also be afraid, sad, angry, jealous, frustrated, and any other human emotion.

Transforming negativity refers to our ability to shift negativity into something new and more productive. The next time you find yourself in the grip of negative emotions, try generating some positive emotions to go alongside them. It's hard to feel [EMOTION] right now. Feeling [EMOTION] is part of the human experience. What can I do to make myself happier at this moment? Choose to find the silver lining in the dark clouds. Think of one or two of the biggest challenges you've faced in your life so far - problems that were so difficult you thought you'd never get through them at the time. In hindsight, can you see if anything good came out of the experience? Did you grow as a person, learn something important, find more meaning in your life? Next, think about a challenge you're facing right now. Is there any way to see your problem in a different light? Is there anything positive that might come out of your present circumstances?

Practice appreciating yourself. List ten things about yourself that you like or appreciate. As you write down each quality, see if you can notice any uncomfortable feelings of embarrassment, fear of vanity, or unfamiliarity. If discomfort comes up, remind yourself that you are not claiming you're better than anyone else, nor that you're perfect. You're simply noting the good qualities that you sometimes display.

Practice mindfulness. Mindfulness is about being aware of and present to what is. For instance, during a moment of difficulty, you might feel the urge to jump into action to avoid your true feelings. Instead, mindfulness invites us to observe these feelings and recognize them, non-judgmentally, for what they are. Mindfulness can be a space for practicing the habits of recognition and non-reactivity. Remember that self-awareness and non-reactivity are always available.

CHAPTER 4 KEY TAKEAWAYS:

- Moving away from people-pleasing will require you to get comfortable with your negative emotions instead of avoiding them or pushing them away - self-compassion practices support you in accepting and processing negative emotion and in introducing positive emotion alongside it.
- It is possible to re-wire your brain to more positive and productive thinking, and self-concept using practices of mindfulness, positive affirmations, and visualization.

PART 3: SELF-CARE

CHAPTER 5: HOW DO I PLEASE MYSELF?

In the last section, you discovered how to confront people-pleasing head-on while also learning how to engage with negative emotions safely. You found practices for self-acceptance and techniques for new beliefs, and how to rewire your people-pleasing brain. This section will connect to your own needs and priorities while re-establishing your desires, joy, and passions. You will connect with your values and learn tools to build self-worth and self-efficacy.

In this section, you will:

- Connect to your own needs & set priorities.
- Re-establish your desires, joy, and passions.
- Take back control of your life with habits, rituals, and self-care.
- Establish meaning in your life.
- Gain tools to build self-worth and self-efficacy.

How do I please myself?

People-pleasers devote very little time or energy towards taking care of their health and needs. As a people-pleaser, taking care of others takes priority over their needs to be active, de-stress, sleep well, or even the need to have fun. Taking care of others is not a bad thing. However, you cannot take care of others at the expense of yourself. In reading this book and completing these reflection exercises, you are now turning your focus onto your self-care and ability to turn inward to please yourself! When you take care of yourself, you will have more energy and vitality to share with the world. Taking care of yourself is a crucial component of breaking up with people-pleasing. Practicing healthy habits helps you put your needs first and increases your ability to love yourself. Looking after yourself and taking care of your body isn't selfish. As a recovering people-pleaser, you might have taken care of others' health before your own in the past. It is now time to carve out an excellent plan to keep yourself healthy and full of vitality.

Connect to your own needs & set priorities:

As part of setting boundaries, you need to connect to what is truly essential. Good boundaries and the ability to set priorities in your life will provide you with a sense of safety and control. What are your needs, exactly? When you don't get your own needs met, it can feel like an energy drain. Since you might have been a people-pleaser for a big part of your life, you may have little sense of yourself and your personal needs. A central part of self-care is getting to know yourself and your needs again. This means knowing your innermost feelings, choices, and desires - connecting back to knowing your true self.

Like the other steps of breaking up with people-pleasing, this reconnection to self is a process. Read on for some tangible strategies to help you tap back into your true self, your needs, and your priorities:

Tune in to rediscover your passions. Get quiet and take time to be still and listen. Many people don't know themselves because getting quiet and listening can be uncomfortable. Realize who you are, not who you want to be. What do you love? What are you drawn to? Who are you when no one is looking? Find what you are passionate about. Pay attention when it comes to your energy and excitement levels. Focus more on your passion, and you will begin to understand yourself better.

Here are some questions to consider that might help you uncover your true desires, joy, and passions:

- Who are you when no one is looking?
- What do you love to do? What comes easily to you?
- What are qualities you enjoy expressing in the world?
- What is your heart telling you?
- Where do you wish you could go right now?
- What are some of the times in your life you experienced great joy?
- When have you been most proud of yourself?

- When have you experienced extreme happiness? What were you doing?
- What fulfills you?
- What club would you join?
- What group do you like being a part of?
- Who are you envious of? What are they doing?

Pinpoint what you need. Simply ask yourself: What am I feeling? What do I need in this moment? What am I wanting? Ask others for feedback if you are finding this difficult. If you don't know yourself, hearing what other people say about you can be eye-opening. Ask others who you trust questions to understand how they see you. (For example, "What strengths do you see in me?") These questions will help you find yourself again. Differentiate yourself from others as an independent individual. Take notice of how you are unique, special, and different. It is essential to pinpoint your own specific needs and value yourself enough to make your needs a priority.

Take time for self-care. Make time for an activity that you enjoy. Do things that make you feel satisfied with your work, home, health, or other areas that you value. Make a conscious effort to build these into your life. Actively look for ways to make time for you and your needs. You can organize or change your schedule to make self-care happen. Part of this is saying 'no' to others. Learning to say no can take practice. At the end of the day, you need to remember that you matter — your needs matter.

Take back control of your life with habits, rituals, and self-care. Practice healthy habits such as eating a healthy diet, exercising regularly, and doing things that make your body feel good and alive. Do activities that bring you joy. Listen to music that delights you and move your body. Active living and movement can help you feel good physically, mentally, emotionally, and spiritually. Movement is a form of self-care - your body wants to move! Emotions are a form of energy that moves through our bodies, and therefore our bodies play a big part in emotional regulation. It becomes essential as a part of your self-care to move this energy through your body. Any form of movement is good - and there are so many ways to move your body: take a walk, dance, stretch, shake it, jump, go for a run. The possibilities are endless.

Take time to rest and be quiet. It is common for people-pleasers to be exhausted, especially when you strive to be all things to all people. Sometimes we are tired from being on the go for many hours of the day. Part of self-care is taking time to rest without apology. We often think sleep or rest is weak or lazy. This is simply false - rest is a basic human need. You deserve to rest. You need to sleep. We fill our lives with endless activities, especially when we are trying to please and impress others. Build rest into your day proactively, before you begin to feel burnt out and lifeless. We often take pride in being able to say "I am so busy." However, the more we are able to rest and nourish ourselves, the more powerful we are in our lives. Rest plays a significant role in replenishing and regulating the nervous system. After making a decision to prioritize rest, you must determine what form of rest is best for you. Experiment with different ways of getting quiet and resting to find what fits best for you.

Get outside. Nature is a powerful and often underrated tool for self-care. Countless studies prove the powerful benefits of spending time in nature. Spending time in nature lowers stress, promotes happiness, and improves productivity. There are many ways to get outside and experience the benefits of nature - whether you walk, hike, do yoga, spend time in your garden, or simply breathe fresh air or feel the sunshine on your skin.

Bedtime rituals and mediation. Creating rhythms and rituals in your days can help create a sense of greater control of your life. Bedtime routines and positive sleep hygiene will help you to feel better and cope with stress more effectively. Research demonstrates that forming good habits of beneficial routines for good sleep is vital for your physical and mental health. Sleep hygiene refers to daily practices and habits that promote consistent, uninterrupted, healthy sleep. Some good bedtime rituals might be:

taking a warm bath or shower, personal hygiene self-care, turning down the lights, stopping screen use a couple of hours before bed, blue light blocking glasses, writing in a gratitude journal, guided or self-meditation, gentle yoga, paced breathing, mindfulness, and relaxation music. Creating a relaxing pre-bed routine and planning a consistent wake-up time will help promote predictability around your sleep, resulting in more effective rest.

Connect with loved ones. Another important piece of the self-care puzzle is spending time with loved ones and supportive figures in your life. Make a point to catch up and socialize with loved ones often. A good laugh and time spent together with others can feed us energetically and mentally. It is easy to lose yourself in your life and forget the outside world - making a conscious effort to be a friend and talk to friends is essential. Human connection brings many benefits to our lives, such as giving us a sense of belonging and identity, and it can also be a therapeutic support system. Science has shown social connection is a core psychological need to feel satisfied with life.

Create new habits. Making seemingly tiny habit changes can bring you remarkable results. Even the smallest habit changes or improvements can accumulate over time into remarkable results and major changes! It is easy to overestimate the importance of one defining moment and underestimate the value of making minor improvements daily! First, identify the changes you would like to make, then establish the habit you want to adopt, and - most importantly of all - repeat it! Repetition is what will make a new habit stick. Make your new desired habits obvious and make them stand out. Make them attractive and allow yourself to anticipate goodness from the habit change. Make it easy for yourself to take action. Make the new habit satisfying so you will repeat it. What do you want to become? What habits do you want to build into your days?

Establish meaning in your life. Think about what you want for yourself. Many of us fall too easily into being victimized by thoughts and complaints about circumstances rather than orienting towards our dreams, goals, and wishes. It becomes essential to focus on what you do want. Knowing what you want is fundamental to finding your true self and establishing more meaning and purpose. It becomes critical to seek your sense of purpose. This means separating your point of view from others' expectations of you and reconnecting to your power based on your strengths, competencies, and passion in life. Self-care is honouring this personal power and ability to strive for your own desired destiny.

Tools to build self-worth and self-efficacy:

Gratitude - In his book *Thanks: How Practicing Gratitude Can Make You Happier*, Robert Emmons, one of the leading scholars in the positive psychology movement, teaches strategies to cultivate gratitude and embrace all the benefits it brings to our lives. Gratitude is recognizing and acknowledging the goodness in one's life and acknowledging that the sources of this goodness lie partially outside of ourselves (Emmons 2007).

Gratitude is more than a feeling - it is a knowing & awareness that we are the recipients of goodness. Gratitude is remembering the contributions that others have made for the sake of your well-being. Gratitude feels good, so personal happiness becomes the ultimate motivation for gratitude. Gratitude is not just a form of "positive thinking" or a technique of "Happy-ology," but rather a deep abiding recognition and acknowledgement that goodness exists under even the worst that life offers. Gratitude is a chosen attitude. It is an approach to life that can be freely chosen for oneself. Gratitude is a conscious decision. We can sharpen our ability to recognize and acknowledge the giftedness of life.

Gratitude is likely to elevate happiness for several reasons:

- Grateful thinking fosters the savouring of positive life experiences and situations.
- Grateful people extract the maximum possible satisfaction and enjoyment from their circumstances.
- Gratitude practice may directly counteract the effects of hedonic adaptation - the process by which our happiness level returns again and again to a set point despite positive or negative life events. This prevents people from taking the good things in their lives for granted.
- The very act of seeing things as a gift to be grateful for is likely to be beneficial for mood.
- Gratitude strengthens relationships.
- Gratitude enhances our human spirit by adding meaning and purpose to our lives.

Strategies for Practicing Gratitude:

- Keep a gratitude journal. At the end of each day, write down 3-5 things that you are grateful for.
- Incorporate gratitude into prayers and other rituals & rhythms.
- Listen to gratitude-focused guided meditations.
- Tune in to your senses: what do I taste, smell, see, hear, feel? Notice and express gratitude for these sensory experiences.
- Express gratitude verbally in your relationships.
- Flex your gratitude muscle by looking out for things to be grateful for throughout your day - this will shift your orientation and help you notice things to feel grateful for more consistently.

Focus on appreciation. Research confirms that good things happen to the minds, hearts, and bodies of people who feel appreciated. In *The Power of Appreciation*, Noelle Nelson and Jeannine Calaba state that appreciation is the energy you use proactively. Appreciation has two main components: gratitude (as described earlier in the chapter) and valuing - an active, conscious choice to value people or things. (Nelson & Calaba 2003). Become an appreciator and start by appreciating life itself: become opportunity-minded vs. problem-minded. Develop an appreciative state of mind and apply that appreciation toward your loved ones and, even more importantly, toward yourself.

Take time to savour & reminisce. Take a 15-30 minute pleasure walk outside. This walk's goal is to notice as many pleasant things as possible so that you are generating a positive, pleasurable frame of mind. How many happy, beautiful, or inspiring things can you notice while you're walking? Positive psychology uses the concept of savouring to maximize the potential benefit of positive experiences and emotions. The idea of savouring and reminiscing is about being mindfully engaged and aware of your positive feelings. Savour the good.

Appreciate and accept yourself. Self-acceptance is not an automatic default state that you might find yourself in. Accepting ourselves precisely as we are can be majorly challenging at times. True self-acceptance means accepting all of your attributes, positive or negative - this is often a challenging proposition. Accepting yourself, including your flaws and mistakes, is not about condoning any harmful or negative behaviour - but rather embracing and appreciating the person you are. Look at this as self-acceptance training. Acceptance of oneself and one's reality, flaws and all, is an essential building block of many recovery programs. It is also essential for those recovering from people-pleasing.

REFLECTION EXERCISE:

List ten things about yourself that you like or appreciate. As you write down each quality, see if you can notice any uncomfortable feelings of embarrassment, fear of vanity, or unfamiliarity. If discomfort comes up, remind yourself that you are not claiming you're better than anyone else or that you're perfect. You're simply noting the good qualities that you sometimes display.

_____

_____

_____

_____

_____

CHAPTER 5 KEY TAKEAWAYS:

- As a people-pleaser, you may find yourself disconnected from or unaware of your own needs. Getting clear on your own needs and the things that bring you joy is key to pleasing yourself.
- Implementing a gratitude practice will help you become more aware of the things in your life that bring you joy and energy to prioritize and protect those things consistently.

CHAPTER 6:
HOW DO I THRIVE IN MY RELATIONSHIPS?

In the previous chapters, we've engaged in plenty of self-reflection on the phenomenon of people-pleasing, why we do it, what needs it is meeting for us, and how it shows up in our lives. We've discussed ways to interrupt your people-pleasing behaviour and how to focus intensely on pleasing yourself.

In this chapter, we're going to focus on our relationships with *others*. We'll discuss strategies you can employ in your relationships to have meaningful, intimate, fulfilling connections while also prioritizing and honouring your own needs.

In this chapter, you will:

- Reflect on your relationship to boundaries and boundary-setting.
- Identify strategies for strengthening communication and setting boundaries in your relationships with others so you can maintain connections without abandoning yourself.
- Create a plan for setting boundaries and how to respond when a boundary is violated.

As we think about our people-pleasing patterns and how to approach our relationships differently, we do a significant amount of thought work and self-reflection - and that foundation is critically important to our growth. The real test comes in applying all of this self-reflection to how we show up in relationships. The way that this ends up looking in practice is through our interpersonal communication and boundaries in our relationships. This chapter is designed to walk you through some concrete, straightforward strategies to help you through that and to support you in building some new, healthier practices to thrive in your relationships.

The first thing we need to do to increase the health of our relationships is to get comfortable naming and owning our feelings and needs.

When we think about boundaries and communication, we tend to think a lot about saying "no" and setting limits, which can often feel very dramatic and even scary! Many of us associate boundary-setting with a sense of loss. There is a fear that setting a boundary will result in a loss of intimacy or the end of a relationship. This process can sound pretty straightforward and intuitive, but we know that this is not always easy, especially if you're someone who has lost touch with or become disconnected from your feelings and your own needs. That is important, and we'll get there later in this chapter. But before that, a foundational part of setting boundaries is first to simply get more comfortable naming what you're feeling - or at a minimum, being able to recognize it. This part is not optional and *must* come first - it's the foundation upon which every other boundary-setting practice rests.

The reality is that when a boundary or a value is violated, we know it. We *feel* it in our bodies. Think about the last time someone breached a boundary for you or did something that felt hurtful, like they weren't meeting your needs or weren't considering your feelings. Take a minute to think about what that *felt* like - emotionally, mentally, and physically in your body. Take a minute to write it down if you need to.

The key here is just being able to describe and ultimately recognize this feeling. When you're able to identify the feeling of a boundary being crossed and know when it's happening, then you'll be able to map back the things that led to and ultimately triggered that feeling. You'll become deeply familiar with the feeling, and eventually, you'll be able to put words to it. You'll be able to name it when you notice it creeping in. You'll be able to detect patterns of events, behaviours, or interactions that often lead to those feelings and draw connections. Begin tracking these moments in some way, either mentally or writing it down somewhere. This first step is still really self-focused and doesn't necessarily require anything externally. However, it can be beneficial to have someone you trust, who knows that you are on this journey, who you can talk through these experiences with, and who can help you process and name your feelings without fear of judgment or shame. Recognizing how we feel when boundaries are violated is critical because the next practice is where you turn these things outward. We're going to begin to communicate our feelings, needs, and boundaries. It is worth saying again.

Communicate our feelings, needs, and boundaries clearly and directly.

Yes, this is the part that can feel the most uncomfortable and scary. You knew we would get here eventually - this is the transformative relational work of breaking up with people-pleasing. This is where the rubber meets the road!

This is also the moment where we hear our inner voice asking:

What if I set a boundary, and someone gets angry at me?
What if they yell at me?
What if they don't respect me when I say no?
What if they laugh at me?

Sound familiar? These are some of the fears from chapter three that pushed us into the pattern of people-pleasing in the first place! But we aren't allowing those fears to hold us back anymore.

If the idea of setting boundaries sounds scary to you, consider this: we often imagine boundary setting as a harsh and dramatic one-time event. Many of us imagine that to set a boundary effectively, we must very loudly and aggressively proclaim, "this is my boundary" in a way that upsets and hurts people - like a scene straight out of a movie!

Guess what? It doesn't have to be that way most of the time.

Of course, there will be times when someone isn't listening to you or honouring you, moments when someone gets upset or feels frustrated, and moments when you have to be straightforward with others when you set a boundary.

But a *lot* of the time, boundary-setting can be a much more relaxed conversation than you think (and it will likely feel even less dramatic or different than usual to the person you are speaking to than it will to you).

Having trouble imagining what it would look like for you to set a boundary? Picture this:

- If you're somebody who usually says, "I'm fine!" even when you're not, boundary-setting can look like saying, "You know, I'm feeling a little bit low-energy today" when someone asks how you're doing.
- It can look like someone inviting you to do something and saying, "Oh no, unfortunately, I can't join, but thanks so much for inviting me!"
- It can be you saying, "If you don't mind, I'd prefer we talk about something else," if you're not comfortable with a particular topic.

And yes, you will probably need to communicate boundaries that feel higher stakes than these examples at some point. Like any habit you're hoping to create, boundary-setting is a muscle that you have to build. It feels uncomfortable not only because you're afraid of how people will respond, but also just because you aren't used to doing it! You aren't used to having these types of conversations - so the way to get more comfortable is to practice! But when you are first practicing boundary-setting as a brand-new skill, the lower-stakes and lower-intensity boundaries are a great place to start.

Does the idea of boundary-setting bring up a fear of being perceived as mean, cold, or unkind? This fear makes total sense for a people-pleaser focused on helping others feel good and taken care of! On the face of it, it can feel like boundary setting is revoking your kindness and care, but in fact it's quite the opposite! The critical thing to remember is that by clearly communicating your boundaries, you invite someone to treat you the way you want and need to be treated. You show people what will help you feel the most loved and supported, not ask them to guess or read your mind. This practice isn't necessarily cold or without care, warmth, or empathy. It does not necessarily have to feel like building a wall or creating distance! Healthy boundary-setting is a way of making a bid for meaningful connection - a connection that feels good and fulfilling for everyone involved.

In particular for this boundary-setting practice, it will be essential to identify a person in your life who is safe to practice boundary-setting with. This safe place could be with a supportive person who is generally more attuned to your needs, or it could be someone you feel comfortable saying, "I'm trying to work on some new practices to communicate more clearly and set boundaries in my relationships, would you be open to me trying some of those things with you?" Just like with anything else, implementing all of these new practices at once in every single one of your relationships across the board is going to feel overwhelming. But suppose you can introduce it into a few close relationships at first, with people you trust, and start to incorporate it into your habits and practices there. In that case, that will make all of this feel more manageable and sustainable.

We do have some bad news, though.

After you start to practice these things, you get attuned to your own needs and what it feels like to have your boundaries violated. You begin communicating your boundaries - someone's going to break them.

Sorry! We wish this weren't true, but it is. This inconsistency is what it is to be a human in a relationship with other humans. Someone's going to disregard your feelings, or they're going to violate a boundary, and you're going to have to figure out how to address that. so, the next practice is making sure that we:

Decide and commit to consequences for boundary violations ahead of time.

When setting boundaries with someone, we need to be clear - both with that person and with ourselves.

There are a couple of reasons for this. One is because we want to make it clear to that other person what will happen if they don't respect our boundaries. We want it to be clear enough that there is no room for speculation or misinterpretation. But we also do this because we know that, as humans, we don't do our best decision-making in times of stress, pain, or frustration. We have to decide ahead of time and commit to maintaining and honouring that in the moment, so that there's no question about what we do. We've communicated it to that person, and they chose to violate the boundary anyway. We made clear what was going to happen, and now we follow through with it.

A very concrete example of this:

Let's say that you tell a friend they can borrow your car, but at the time of your agreement, you specifically asked that your friend doesn't bring any food in the car because the smell of food lingering in your vehicle bothers you. You tell them that you're happy to have them borrow the car, but you just ask that they respect that boundary, and if they can't, they won't get to use your vehicle again.

Now, if that person borrows your car and brings it back to you and it smells like french fries, and you find french fries under the seat, you know that they have violated your boundary. You're going to be frustrated in the moment. You're likely to feel angry that they didn't respect your boundary. You might not feel great about saying something to them at that moment. You might wonder, "ugh, how do I bring this up to them?"

However, since you decided and communicated the consequences ahead of time, you don't have to think about addressing this. You can say to this person who borrowed your car, "As we talked about, I asked that you not bring food into my car, but it looks like you did eat in my car. I'm not going to be able to let you borrow my car again."

This strategy works for any type of boundary. Examples of boundaries with belongings just feel easier to understand and a little less abstract than things to do with feelings, communication, or relationships. What's critical here is not the specific boundary itself but naming the boundary and the consequences ahead of time, when we aren't in that intense emotional space when we've just had our boundary violated.

One important thing to remember here is that what makes this stick is the follow-through. You have to name the consequence ahead of time, yes, but then you have to honour it and follow through with it. Which is why the last practice we'll talk about for introducing healthy communication and boundary setting is the practice of:

Staying consistent and unapologetic about your boundaries.

This is important if our boundary-setting is going to be a sustainable practice. If we feel guilty and crappy about having set boundaries, we aren't likely to stay consistent and hold firm to our boundaries.

The key here is remembering that setting boundaries isn't anything to feel sorry for. When we are so used to making sure other people get their needs met and don't communicate about our own, having boundaries and expressing our needs and setting limits with people can feel wrong at times. It may feel counterintuitive and even like something we should apologize for.

To make these practices sustainable, you can not be sorry for setting boundaries.

Remember what we said earlier: setting boundaries is not creating disconnection, intentionally hurting anyone, or putting people down. It is not stepping all over or violating other people's boundaries.

Another truth that has become clear in this work is that the common fear of people-pleasers is that if we stop people-pleasing, we'll make other people feel the same pain of rejection we've felt. We fear that we'll make other people think they were walked over, feel invisible, feel neglected, or feel like their needs don't matter.

You must understand that is *not* what you are doing by communicating your needs and setting boundaries. Setting a boundary for yourself is *not* an indictment of someone else's worth or inherent goodness. By setting boundaries, we are making clear how we need to be treated to feel valued, loved and supported. We are giving people clear, simple-to-follow instructions for loving us well in a way that invites them in closer. We aren't building a wall - we are building a solid and supportive bridge.

There's nothing, absolutely nothing, to feel sorry for about that.

To recap, there are four new practices that we're going to begin to implement to thrive in our relationships:

1. Get comfortable naming and owning your feelings.
2. Communicate ysour feelings, needs, and boundaries clearly and directly.
3. Decide and commit to consequences for boundary violations ahead of time.
4. Stay consistent and unapologetic about your boundaries.

REFLECTION EXERCISE:

Think about a time that your boundaries were violated, or you felt that your needs were disregarded. How did that feel? What thoughts came up for you? How did it feel in your body?

Name one boundary that you know you need to set. Be as specific as possible.

Write out the consequences if someone violates this boundary.

How will you communicate the boundary and the consequence of violating it?

Name a trusted person that you can practice boundary-setting conversations.

_____

_____

_____

_____

_____

CHAPTER 6 KEY TAKEAWAYS:

- Healthy relationships require us to state and uphold our boundaries.
- Setting healthy boundaries includes naming and owning our needs, communicating those needs, identifying what will happen if our needs are not met, and sticking to our stated consequences.
- Setting and maintaining boundaries can be challenging, but it is the single most incredible tool you can use as a people-pleaser to transform your relationships.

CONCLUSION: WHERE DO WE GO FROM HERE?

In this book, you have learned:

- What people-pleasing looks like.
- Why humans become people-pleasers.
- Why you engage in people-pleasing behaviours.
- How to stop people-pleasing behaviours.
- How to please yourself.
- How to thrive in your relationships.

By learning about these concepts, gaining these new tools, and engaging with the reflective exercises throughout this book, you have taken the first few significant steps in breaking up with people-pleasing. When you have lived for so long with people-pleasing as your default programming, you might notice your old people-pleasing tendencies creeping back into your life in small ways - particularly when you feel tired or stressed. However, just like a toxic ex-partner, people-pleasing will continue to be there even after you've said goodbye.

This shift does not mean that your progress is for nothing! Don't throw in the towel here. Keep going and keep practicing.

Remember that recognizing this behaviour as people-pleasing in the first place is progress in and of itself! You may have picked up this book not even realizing that certain behaviours were examples of people-pleasing; now you are armed with the knowledge that will help you recognize these patterns if they re-emerge and respond accordingly.

Wherever your people-pleasing journey takes you, remember that self-compassion is central to healing patterns of people-pleasing. If you cannot appreciate, value, and tune in to your own needs, it is challenging to recognize when you abandon those needs to serve someone else's.

When you find yourself struggling, remind yourself of the questions and techniques in this book. You may need to pull it out now and again and utilize some of the reflection questions or reread some chapters to reconnect you with your own needs - that's okay. Allow yourself that grace.

Healing is not always linear, but it is always worthwhile. Exercise the same compassion for yourself that you would offer someone else. And most importantly - remember that you are not making this journey alone.

REFERENCES

Adams, Marilee. (2009). *Change your questions, change your life: 10 powerful tools for life and work.* San Francisco: Berrett-Koehler Publishers.

Braiker, Harriet. (2001). *The Disease to Please: Curing the People-Pleasing Syndrome.* New York: McGraw-Hill.

Beattie, Melody. (1992). *Codependent no more: how to stop controlling others and start caring for yourself.* Center City, MN: Hazelden

Duckworth A, Gendler T, Gross J. Situational strategies for self-control. *Perspectives on Psychological Science.* 2016; 11(1):35–55.

Duhigg, Charles. (2014). *The power of habit: why we do what we do in life and business.* New York: Random House.

Dweck, Carol S. (2006). *Mindset: The new psychology of success.* New York: Random House.

Emmons, Robert A. (2007). *Thanks!: how the new science of gratitude can make you happier.* Boston: Houghton Mifflin Co.

Fredrickson, Barbara. (2010). *Positivity: Groundbreaking Research to Release Your Inner Optimist and Thrive.* OneWorld Publications.

Gollwitzer, P. M. (1999). Implementation intentions: Strong effects of simple plans. *American Psychologist*, 54(7), 493–503.

Hanson, Rick. (2013). *Hardwiring Happiness: The New Brain Science of Contentment, Calm, & Confidence.* New York: Harmony Books.

Neff, Kristin. (2011). Self-compassion: the proven power of being kind to yourself. New York: William Morrow.

Nelson, Noelle C. & Calaba, Jeannine L. (2003). *The Power of Appreciation: The Key to a Vibrant Life.* New York: Simon & Schuster.

Schwartz, Jeffrey & Gladding, Rebecca. (2011). *You are not your brain: the 4-step solution for changing bad habits, ending unhealthy thinking, and taking control of your life.* New York: Avery.

ABOUT THE AUTHORS

AUBREE HENDERSON

Aubree Henderson is a self-worth coach, writer, and podcast host based in Brooklyn, New York. A native midwesterner, Aubree earned a bachelor's degree in Psychology and Gender & Women's Studies at the University of Illinois at Urbana-Champaign, followed by a M.Ed. in Human Development & Mental Health Counseling from Vanderbilt University in Nashville, Tennessee. Aubree has applied her knowledge and skills as an individual and group counselor, a classroom instructor, workshop facilitator, sex educator, nonprofit leader, and podcast host. She received her professional coaching certification in 2019 and has been coaching individuals and groups on self-worth and communication ever since. In addition to coaching clients 1-on-1 and in small groups, she also hosts a weekly self-worth & advice podcast called Ask Aubree and shares her insights on Instagram @ahhhhbree.

Aubree is a lover of plants, poetry, the Enneagram, hair dye, rescue animals, and iced coffee. She lives in Brooklyn with her wife, Laura. They are foster moms to three amazing kids.

ANDREA SEYDEL

Andrea Seydel is a Positive Psychology Practitioner, Certified Life Coach and 7-time best-selling author. She specializes in resilience training, non-violent communication, and well-being. She earned her bachelor's degree in Psychology with post-graduate training in Positive Psychology. Andrea currently applies her knowledge working in the community of addiction recovery and resilience, as a writer, and the host of The Live Life Happy podcast and show.

Andrea offers positive psychology coaching services, writing workshops, book coaching services, and unconventional book clubs. Andrea is lovingly called the "Book Doula" as she helps individuals painlessly give birth to books. She is the founder of Live Life Happy Publishing and is the proud mother of two grown children. She lives in Canada.

Live Life Happy-Publishing
Helping people painlessly give birth to books that change lives.

Dear Reader,

Thank you for purchasing this unique book and joining the **Live Life Happy Community** of readers. We are a publishing company that is committed to bringing positive, supportive and well-being-enhancing books to life.

As a welcoming gift, we'd like to offer you free access to the **Live Life Happy Book Vault**, which is full of resources and support to help you live a flourishing life. You can gain access here:
www.andreaseydel.com.

Finally, if you or someone you know has been thinking about writing a book, sharing a message or gaining credibility in an industry, I can help you painlessly give birth to your book. As a book doula and founder of LLH Publishing, I help make author ***book-writing dreams come true***. Best of all, these books are changing lives, and your message can help others too. So don't hesitate to reach out and set up a Book Chat, and please stay in touch!

Sincerely,
Andrea Seydel
(The Book Doula)

Questions? Comments? Contact me at
andrea.livelifehappy@gmail.com.

P.S. Books Change Lives: Whose life will you touch with yours?

www.ingramcontent.com/pod-product-compliance
Lightning Source LLC
Chambersburg PA
CBHW070556160426
43199CB00014B/2522